fashions
to flaunt
crocheted with
Noro
Yarns™

fashions
to flaunt
crocheted with
Noro
Yarns™

credits

EDITOR Connie Ellison
CREATIVE DIRECTOR Brad Snow
PUBLISHING SERVICES DIRECTOR Brenda Gallmeyer

ASSISTANT EDITOR Judy Crow
ASSISTANT ART DIRECTOR Nick Pierce
COPY SUPERVISOR Deborah Morgan
COPY EDITORS Emily Carter, Sam Schneider
TECHNICAL EDITOR Mary Ann Frits

PRODUCTION ARTIST SUPERVISOR Erin Brandt
COVER & BOOK DESIGN Greg Smith
PRODUCTION ARTISTS Glenda Chamberlain, Edith Teegarden
PRODUCTION ASSISTANTS Marj Morgan, Judy Neuenschwander

PHOTOGRAPHY SUPERVISOR Tammy Christian
PHOTOGRAPHY Scott Campbell
PHOTO STYLISTS Martha Coquat

contents

light layers vest

SKILL LEVEL

EASY

SIZES
Instructions given fit X-large; changes for 2X-large are in [ ].

FINISHED GARMENT SIZES
Bottom width: 43 [50] inches
Length at center back: 20 [22] inches

MATERIALS

- Noro Silk Garden Sock super fine (sock) weight yarn (3 oz/328 yds/100g per ball): 3 balls #272 grays/lime/brown
- Sizes G/6/4mm and I/9/5.5mm crochet hooks or size needed to obtain gauge
- Tapestry needle

1 SUPER FINE

GAUGE
With size I hook: 4 shells = 4 inches

Take time to check gauge.

PATTERN NOTES
Weave in ends as work progresses.

Join with slip stitch as indicated unless otherwise stated.

Vest is worked in one piece beginning at right front, across back to left front.

SPECIAL STITCH
Shell: (Sc, ch 3, 3 dc) in indicated st or sp.

VEST
Row 1: With size I hook, ch 92 [102], **shell** *(see Special Stitch)* in 2nd ch from hook, *sk next 4 chs, shell in next st, rep from * across to last 5 chs, sk next 4 chs, sc in last ch, turn. *(18 [20] shells, 1 sc)*

Row 2: Ch 1, shell in first sc, shell in ch-3 sp of each shell across to last shell, sc in ch-3 sp of last shell, turn.

Rows 3–28 [3–32]: Rep row 2.

FIRST ARMHOLE SHAPING
Row 29 [33]: Ch 1, shell in first sc, shell in ch-3 sp of each of next 3 shells, ch 40 [50], sk next 8 [10] shells, shell in ch-3 sp of each of next 6 shells, sc in ch-3 sp of last shell, turn.

Row 30 [34]: Ch 1, shell in first sc, shell in ch-3 sp of each of next 6 shells, sk first 2 chs of next 40 [50] chs, shell in next ch, [sk next 4 chs, shell in next ch] 7 [9] times, shell in ch-3 sp of each of next 3 shells, sc in ch-3 sp of last shell, turn. *(18 [20] shells, 1 sc)*

Rows 31–46 [35–54]: Rep row 2.

2ND ARMHOLE SHAPING
Rows 47 & 48 [55 & 56]: Rep rows 29 [33] and 30 [34].

Rows 49–72 [57–84]: Rep row 2.

At end of last row, fasten off.

OUTER EDGING
Row 1: With 1 long edge at top and with size G hook, **join** *(see Pattern Notes)* yarn in edge of first row at right-hand edge, *ch 1, sc in same sp, ch 1, sk next row, sc in next row, taking care to keep edge flat, rep from * across, turn.

Row 2: Ch 2, (sc, ch 1) in each ch-1 sp across. Fasten off.

Continued on page 41

bobble scarf

SKILL LEVEL

EASY

SIZE

6 inches x 65 inches

MATERIALS

- Noro Silk Garden super fine (sock) weight yarn (3 oz/328 yds/ 100g per ball):
    1 ball yarn color of choice
- Size E/4/3.5mm crochet hook or size needed to obtain gauge
- Tapestry needle

1
SUPER FINE

GAUGE

18 sts = 4 inches

Take time to check gauge.

PATTERN NOTES

Weave in ends as work progresses.

This is a lattice scarf with 1 bobble worked at end of each row. There is an increase at one end and a decrease at the other end so that the scarf has a diagonal shape.

SPECIAL STITCH

Bobble: Holding back last lp of each tr on hook, 7 tr in indicated st, yo and draw through all 8 lps on hook.

SCARF

Row 1: Ch 50, dc in 6th ch from hook, *ch 1, sk next ch, dc in next ch, rep from * across, ch 20, turn. (*23 ch sps*)

Row 2: **Bobble** (*see Special Stitch*) in 5th ch from hook, sc in same ch, ch 15, (dc, ch 1, dc) in first dc, *ch 1, sk next ch, dc in next dc, rep from * across to last 2 dc, **dc dec** (*see Stitch Guide*) in last 2 dc, ch 20, turn.

Row 3: (Bobble, sc) in 5th ch from hook, ch 15, dc dec in first 2 dc, work in lattice pattern to last st, (dc, ch 1, dc) in last st, turn.

Rep rows 2 and 3 alternately until piece measures 65 inches from beg. At end of last row, fasten off. ■

aztec shawl

SKILL LEVEL
■■□□
EASY

SIZE
26 inches x 67 inches

MATERIALS
- Noro Silk Garden Sock super fine (sock) weight yarn (3 oz/328 yds/100g per ball): 3 balls #241 blues/greens/purples

- Size G/6/4mm crochet hook or size needed to obtain gauge
- Tapestry needle

GAUGE
16 sts = 4 inches

Take time to check gauge.

PATTERN NOTES
Weave in ends as work progresses.

Join with slip stitch as indicated unless otherwise stated.

Chain-4 at beginning of row counts as a double crochet and chain-1 space unless otherwise stated.

SPECIAL STITCH
Cluster (cl): Draw up lp in indicated st, sk next st, draw up lp in next st, yo and draw through all 3 lps on hook.

SHAWL
Row 1 (RS): Ch 29, 3 dc in 6th ch from hook, ch 1, (sk next 3 chs, 3 dc in next ch, ch 1) 5 times, sk next 2 chs, dc in last ch, turn. *(6 groups of 3 dc)*

Row 2: Ch 3, (3 dc, ch 1) in each ch-1 sp across, dc in 3rd ch of beg 5 sk chs, turn. *(7 groups of 3 dc)*

Row 3: Ch 4 *(see Pattern Notes)*, sk next 3 dc, (3 dc, ch 1) in each ch-1 sp across, dc in 3rd ch of beg ch-3. *(6 groups of 3 dc)*

Rows 4–7: [Rep rows 2 and 3 alternately] twice.

Row 8: Ch 3, (3 dc, ch 1) in each ch-1 sp across to last ch-1 sp, 3 dc in last ch-1 sp, ch 26, turn.

Row 9: 3 dc in 6th ch from hook, (sk next 3 chs, 3 dc in next ch, ch 1) 5 times, (3 dc, ch 1) in each ch sp across, dc in 3rd ch of beg ch-3, turn. *(12 groups of 3 dc)*

Row 10: Ch 3, (3 dc, ch 1) in each ch-1 sp across, dc in 3rd ch of beg ch-3, turn.

Row 11: Ch 4, sk next 3 dc, (3 dc, ch 1) in each ch-1 sp across, dc in 3rd ch of beg ch-3, turn.

Rows 12–15: [Rep rows 10 and 11 alternately] twice.

Rows 16 & 17: Rep rows 8 and 9. *(18 groups at end of row 17)*

Rows 18–23: [Rep rows 10 and 11 alternately] 3 times.

Rows 24 & 25: Rep rows 8 and 9. *(24 groups at end of row 25)*

Rows 26–93: [Rep rows 10 and 11 alternately] 34 times.

Row 94: Ch 3, (3 dc, ch 1) in each of next 18 ch-1 sps, 3 dc in next ch-1 sp, leaving rem ch sps unworked, turn. *(19 groups of 3 dc)*

Row 95: Ch 4, (3 dc in next ch-1 sp, ch 1) 18 times, dc in 3rd ch of beg ch-3, turn.

Continued on page 41

dolman sleeve lacy shrug

SKILL LEVEL

□■□□
EASY

SIZE
One size fits large–X-large

MATERIALS
- Noro Silk Garden Sock super fine (sock) weight yarn (3 oz/328 yds/100g per ball): 3 balls #241 blues/greens/purples
- Size F/5/3.75mm crochet hook or size needed to obtain gauge
- Tapestry needle
- ⅔ yd ⅛-inch-wide elastic

GAUGE
4 shells and 7 rows = 4 inches

Take time to check gauge.

PATTERN NOTES
Weave in ends as work progresses.

Join with slip stitch as indicated unless otherwise stated.

Chain-4 at beginning of row counts as a double crochet and a chain-1 sp unless otherwise stated.

SPECIAL STITCHES
V-st: (Dc, ch 3, dc) in indicated sp.

Shell: 4 dc in indicated sp.

SHRUG
BACK
Make 2.

Row 1: Beg at sleeve edge and working to back center seam, ch 37, (dc, ch 3, dc) in 6th ch from hook, *sk next 3 chs, **V-st** (see Special Stitches) in next ch, rep from * to last 3 chs, sk next 2 chs, dc in last ch, turn. *(8 V-sts)*

Row 2: Ch 4 (see Pattern Notes), [**shell** (see Special Stitches) in next ch-3 sp, ch 1] across to sp formed by beg 5 sk chs, dc in sp formed by beg 5 sk chs, turn. *(8 shells)*

Row 3: Ch 6, dc in next ch-1 sp, V-st in each rem ch-1 sp across to last ch-1 sp, V-st in last ch-1 sp, turn.

Row 4: Ch 4, [shell in next ch-3 sp, ch 1] across to ch-6 sp, (shell, ch 1, dc) in ch-6 sp, turn. *(9 shells)*

Rows 5–28: Rep [rows 3 and 4 alternately] 12 times. *(21 shells at end of last row)*

Row 29: Ch 5, dc in next ch-1 sp, [sk next shell, V-st in next ch-1 sp] across to last ch-1 sp, (dc, ch 2, dc) in last ch-1 sp, turn.

Row 30: Ch 3, 2 dc in next ch-2 sp, ch 1, [shell in next ch-3 sp, ch 1] across to last ch-5 sp, 3 dc in last ch-5 sp, turn.

Row 31: Ch 3, sk next 2 dc, V-st in each ch-1 sp across to last 3 dc, sk next 2 dc, dc in last dc, turn.

Row 32: Ch 4, [shell in next ch-3 sp, ch 1] across to turning ch-3, dc in the top of turning ch, turn.

Row 33: Ch 5, dc in next ch-1 sp, V-st in each rem ch-1 sp across to last ch-1 sp, (dc, ch 2, dc) in last ch-1 sp, turn.

Row 34: Ch 3, 2 dc in next ch-1 sp, ch 1, [shell in next ch-3 sp, ch 1] across to last ch-5 sp, 3 dc in last ch-5 sp. Fasten off.

Continued on page 42

crisscross vest

SKILL LEVEL

EASY

SIZE
One size fits most

MATERIALS
- Noro Silk Garden Sock super fine (sock) weight yarn (3 oz/328 yds/100g per ball): 3 balls #279 browns/blues/deep rose
- Size G/6/4mm crochet hook or size needed to obtain gauge
- Tapestry needle

1 SUPER FINE

GAUGE
6 V-sts = 4 inches

Take time to check gauge.

PATTERN NOTES
Weave in ends as work progresses.

Chain-3 at beginning of row counts as a double crochet unless otherwise stated.

SPECIAL STITCH
V-st: (Dc, ch 1, dc) in indicated sp.

VEST
FRONT/BACK
Make 2.

Row 1 (RS): Ch 83, **V-st** (*see Special Stitch*) in 6th ch from hook, *sk next 2 chs, V-st in next ch, rep from * across to last 2 chs, sk next ch, dc in last ch, turn. (*26 V-sts*)

Row 2: Ch 3 (*see Pattern Notes*), V-st in each ch-1 sp across, dc in sp formed by beg 5 sk chs, turn.

Row 3: Ch 3, V-st in each of first 7 ch-1 sps, 2 V-sts in each of next 12 ch-1 sps, V-st in each of last 7 ch-1 sps, dc in 3rd ch of turning ch-3, turn. (*38 V-sts*)

Row 4: Ch 3, V-st in each ch-1 sp across, dc in 3rd ch of turning ch-3, turn.

Row 5: Ch 3, V-st in each ch-1 sp across, dc in 3rd ch of turning ch-3, ch 21, turn.

Row 6: V-st in 6th ch from hook, (sk next 2 chs, V-st in next ch) 5 times, V-st in each ch-1 sp across, dc in 3rd ch of turning ch-3, turn. (*44 V-sts*)

Continued on page 44

15

blue moon wrap

SKILL LEVEL

EASY

SIZE
One size fits most

FINISHED GARMENT SIZE
23 inches x 65 inches

MATERIALS
- Noro Silk Garden Lite light (light worsted) weight yarn (1¾ oz/137 yds/50g per ball): 7 balls #3008 blue/green/purple
- Size E/4/3.5mm crochet hook or size needed to obtain gauge
- Tapestry needle
- Stitch marker

3 LIGHT

GAUGE
(Dc, ch 1) 10 times and 8 rows = 4 inches

Take time to check gauge.

PATTERN NOTES
Weave in ends as work progresses.

Join with slip stitch as indicated unless otherwise stated.

Wrap is worked in one piece beginning at wrist, working sleeve and continuing for the remainder of the wrap.

Chain-4 at beginning of row counts as a double crochet and a chain-1 space unless otherwise stated.

WRAP
Row 1: Ch 60, dc in 6th ch from hook, *ch 1, sk next ch, dc in next ch, rep from * across, turn. (28 ch sps)

Row 2: Ch 4 (see Pattern Notes), dc in same st as beg ch-4, ch 1, sk next ch-1 sp, dc in next dc, *ch 1, sk next ch-1 sp, dc in next dc, rep from * across to last ch-1 sp, ch 1, sk last ch-1 sp, dc in 3rd ch of beg 5 sk chs, turn. (59 ch sps)

Row 3: Ch 4, dc in same st as beg ch-4, ch 1, sk next ch-1 sp, dc in next dc, *ch 1, sk next ch-1 sp, dc in next dc, rep from * across to last ch-1 sp, ch 1, sk last ch-1 sp, dc in 3rd ch of beg ch-4, turn. (59 ch sps)

Rows 4–34: Rep row 3.

Row 35: Ch 4, sk next ch-1 sp, dc in next dc, *ch 1, sk next ch-1 sp, dc in next dc, rep from * across to last ch-1 sp, ch 1, sk last ch-1 sp, dc in 3rd ch of beg ch-4, turn.

Rep row 35 until piece measures 65 inches from beg. At end of last row, fasten off.

ASSEMBLY
Fold piece in half lengthwise and sew first 34 rows to form a sleeve.

OUTER EDGING
Rnd 1: Join (see Pattern Notes) yarn in armhole seam, ch 2, [sc, ch 1] evenly sp to next corner, work (sc, ch 1) twice in corner, [sc, ch 1] evenly sp around rem outer edge to beg ch-2 sp, join in beg ch-2 sp, turn.

Rnd 2: Ch 2, [sc in next ch-1 sp, ch 1] around to last sc, sc in last sc. Fasten off.

SLEEVE EDGING
Rnd 1: Join yarn in sleeve seam, ch 2, [sc, ch 1] evenly sp around sleeve edge to beg ch-2 sp, join in beg ch-2 sp, turn.

Rnd 2: Ch 2, [sc in next ch-1 sp, ch 1] around to beg ch-2 sp, join in beg ch-2 sp, turn.

Rnds 3–5: Rep rnd 2. At end of last rnd, fasten off. ■

forest scarf

SKILL LEVEL

EASY

SIZE

10½ inches x 90 inches

MATERIALS

- Noro Silk Garden Sock
  super fine (sock) weight yarn
  (3 oz/328 yds/100g per ball):
     3 balls #252 black/lime/blue
- Size G/6/4mm crochet hook or size
  needed to obtain gauge
- Tapestry needle

GAUGE

2 shells and 5 rows = 4 inches

Take time to check gauge.

PATTERN NOTES

Weave in ends as work progresses.

Chain-5 at beginning of row counts as a
treble crochet and chain-1 space unless
otherwise stated.

SPECIAL STITCHES

Shell: [Tr, ch 1] 6 times in indicated st, tr in
same st.

Beg half shell: Ch 5 (*see Pattern Notes*), [tr, ch 1]
twice in indicated st, tr in same st.

Half shell: [Tr, ch 1] 3 times in indicated st,
tr in same st.

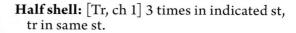

SCARF

Row 1: Ch 61, sc in 2nd ch from hook, (sk next
5 chs, **shell**—*see Pattern Stitches*—in next ch, sk
next 5 chs, sc in next ch) 5 times, turn. (*5 shells*)

Row 2: Beg half shell (*see Special Stitches*) in first
sc, (sc in 4th tr of next shell, shell in next sc)
4 times, sc in 4th tr of next shell, **half shell**
(*see Special Stitches*) in last sc, turn. (*4 shells,
2 half shells*)

Row 3: Ch 1, sc in first tr, (shell in next sc, sc in
4th tr of next shell) 4 times, shell in next sc,
sc in last tr of next half shell, turn. (*5 shells*)

Rep rows 2 and 3 until piece measures 90 inches
from beg. At end of last row, fasten off. ■

slippers

SKILL LEVEL

■■▢▢
EASY

SIZES
Instructions given fit adult small; changes for medium and large are in [ ].

FINISHED SIZES
8-inch sole *(small)* [9-inch sole *(medium)*, 10-inch sole *(large)*]

MATERIALS
- Noro Silk Garden medium (worsted) weight yarn (1¾ oz/110 yds/50g per ball): 3 balls #337 blues/greens/pinks
- Sizes F/5/3.75mm and G/6/4mm crochet hooks or size needed to obtain gauge
- Tapestry needle
- Stitch markers

GAUGE
With size G hook: 8 sts and 18 rnds = 4 inches

PATTERN NOTES
Weave in ends as work progresses.

Join with slip stitch as indicated unless otherwise stated.

SOCK
Make 2.

Note: Sock is worked in continuous rnds. Do not join unless specified. Mark beg of rnd and place markers in 2nd sc of each 3-sc group on both sides. Move markers up each rnd.

Rnd 1: With size G hook, ch 9 [9, 11], 3 sc in 2nd ch from hook, sc in each of next 6 [6, 8] chs, 3 sc in last ch, working on opposite side of foundation ch, sc in each of next 6 [6, 8] chs. *(18 [18, 22] sc)*

Rnd 2: Sc in each sc around.

Rnd 3: Sc in each sc to first marked sc, 3 sc in marked sc, sc in each sc to next marked sc, 3 sc in marked sc, sc in each rem sc. *(22 [22, 26] sc)*

Rnds 4–7 [4–9, 4–15]: [Rep rnds 2 and 3 alternately] 2 [3, 6] times. *(30 [34, 50] sc at end of last rnd)*

Rnd 8 [10, 16]: Rep rnd 2.

Note: Work laid flat should measure 3½ [4¼, 5] inches across.

Rnds 9–23 [11–25, 17–27]: Rep rnd 2.

Note: Mark 8 [8, 12] sts at center front. Remove side markers.

Row 1: Now working in rows, ch 1, sc in each sc to first marker, leaving rem sc unworked, turn.

Row 2: Ch 1, sc in each sc across, turn.

Rows 3–18 [3–20, 3–24]: Rep row 2.

Fold piece in half and sl st through both thicknesses for heel seam. Fasten off.

EDGING
Rnd 1: With size F hook, **join** *(see Pattern Notes)* yarn in heel seam, ch 1, working around Sock opening, sc evenly sp around to beg sc. Do not join.

Rnd 2: Working in **back lps** *(see Stitch Guide)*, sc in each sc around. Do not join.

Rnd 3: Working in back lps, sc in each sc around, **join** *(see Pattern Notes)* in beg sc. Fasten off. ■

SKILL LEVEL

EASY

SIZE
One size fits most

FINISHED GARMENT SIZE
18 inches x 50 inches

MATERIALS
- Noro Kureyon medium (worsted) weight yarn (1¾ oz/110 yds/50g per ball):
    5 balls #170 blue/pink/yellow multi
- Size I/9/5.5mm crochet hook or size needed to obtain gauge
- Tapestry needle

4 MEDIUM

GAUGE
14 sts = 4 inches

Take time to check gauge.

PATTERN NOTES
Weave in ends as work progresses.

Chain-3 at beginning of row counts as a double crochet unless otherwise stated.

Chain-4 at beginning of row counts as a treble crochet unless otherwise stated.

STOLE
Row 1: Ch 59, dc in 4th ch from hook, dc in each rem ch across, turn. *(57 dc)*

Row 2: Ch 4 *(see Pattern Notes)*, tr in each of next 2 dc, *ch 3, sk next 3 dc, tr in each of next 3 dc, rep from * across, turn. *(30 tr, 9 ch-3 sps)*

Row 3: Ch 3 *(see Pattern Notes)*, dc in each tr and in each ch across, turn. *(57 dc)*

Rep rows 2 and 3 until piece measures 50 inches from beg. At end of last row, fasten off. ■

mock cowl scarf

SKILL LEVEL

EASY

FINISHED GARMENT SIZE

16 inches at widest point x 84 inches at longest edge

MATERIALS

- Noro Silk Garden medium (worsted) weight yarn (1¾ oz/110 yds/50g per ball): 3 balls #309 black/orange/lime
- Size P/Q/15mm crochet hook or size needed to obtain gauge
- Tapestry needle

GAUGE

9 sts = 4 inches

Take time to check gauge.

PATTERN NOTE

Weave in ends as work progresses.

SCARF

Row 1 (RS): Ch 4, sc in 2nd ch from hook, 2 sc in next st, 3 sc in last ch, turn. *(6 sc)*

Row 2: Ch 1, working in **front lps** *(see Stitch Guide)*, sc in each sc to last 2 sc, 2 sc in next sc, 3 sc in last sc, turn. *(9 sc)*

Rows 3–26: Rep row 2. *(81 sc at end of last row)*

Row 27: Ch 49, sc in 2nd ch from hook, working in front lps, sc in each rem ch and in each sc across to last 2 sc, 2 sc in next sc, 3 sc in last sc, turn. *(132 sc)*

Row 28: Ch 49, sc in 2nd ch from hook, sc in each rem ch, working in front lps, sc in each sc across, turn. *(180 sc)*

Row 29: Ch 1, working in front lps, sc in each sc across to last sc, sc through both lps of last sc, turn.

Rows 30–41: Rep row 29. At end of last row, fasten off. ◼

lyndalls cardigan

SKILL LEVEL

■□□□
EASY

SIZES

Instructions given fit size small; changes for medium are in [ ].

FINISHED GARMENT MEASUREMENTS

Bust: 32 [36] inches
Length: 28 [28] inches

MATERIALS

- Noro Silk Garden medium (worsted) weight yarn (1¾ oz/110 yds/50g per ball): 9 (10) balls yarn color of choice
- Sizes P/15/10mm and N/13/9mm crochet hooks or size needed to obtain gauge
- Tapestry needle
- Large decorative button

GAUGE

With size P hook: 13 sts = 4 inches

Take time to check gauge.

PATTERN NOTE

Weave in ends as work progresses.

CARDIGAN
BACK

Row 1: With size P hook, ch 56 [60], sc in 4th ch from hook, *ch 1, sk next ch, sc in next ch, rep from * across, turn.

Row 2: Ch 2, *sk next sc, sc in next ch-1 sp, ch 1, rep from * across to sp formed by beg 3 sk chs, sc in same sp, turn.

Row 3: Ch 2, [sc in next ch-1 sp, ch 1] across to ch-2 sp, sc in same ch-2 sp, turn.

Rows 4–47 [4–53]: Rep row 3.

Note: Slip stitches on following row reinforce shoulder seam, which is necessary as this is a dropped shoulder jacket.

SHOULDER SHAPING

Row 48 [54]: Sl st in each of first 12 [14] sts, ch 2, (sk next sc, sc in next ch-1 sp, ch 1) 15 times, sl st in each of last 12 [14] sts. Fasten off.

FRONT
Make 2.

Note: Flip one piece over for 2nd side.

Row 1: With size P hook, ch 30 [34], sc in 4th ch from hook, *ch 1, sk next ch, sc in next ch, rep from * across, turn.

Row 2: Ch 2, [sc in next ch-1 sp, ch 1] across to sp formed by beg 3 sk chs, sc in same sp, turn.

Row 3: Ch 2, [sc in next ch-1 sp, ch 1] across to ch-2 sp, sc in same ch-2 sp, turn.

Rows 4–37 [4–43]: Rep row 3.

Row 38 [44]: Ch 2, sc in first ch-1 sp, (ch 1, sc in next ch-1 sp) 10 [12] times, turn.

Row 39 [45]: Ch 2, **sc dec** *(see Stitch Guide)* in first 2 ch-1 sps, work in pattern across, turn.

Row 40 [46]: Work in pattern.

Row 41 [47]: Ch 2, sc dec in first 2 ch-1 sps, work in pattern across, turn.

Rows 42–47 [48–53]: Work in pattern.

SHOULDER SHAPING

Row 48 [54]: Sl st in each of first 10 [12] sts, ch 2, sc in next ch-1 sp, (ch 1, sc in next ch-1 sp) twice. Fasten off.

Continued on page 45

chain link scarf

SKILL LEVEL

■■□□
EASY

SIZE
16 inches long

MATERIALS
- Noro Silk Garden medium (worsted) weight yarn (1¾ oz/110 yds/50g per ball): 2 balls #84 reds
- Size J/10/6mm Tunisian crochet hook
- Tapestry needle

GAUGE
Gauge is not important for this project.

PATTERN NOTES
Weave in ends as work progresses.

Each Tunisian crochet row consists of a forward pass (FP) and a return pass (RP). The work is always facing forward. While working the forward pass, all of the loops remain on the hook, and for each row of the pattern a return pass is worked as written in the Special Stitches.

SPECIAL STITCHES
Return pass (RP): Yo, draw through first lp on hook, [yo, draw through next 2 lps on hook] across until 1 lp rem on hook. Last lp counts as first st of next row.

Tunisian Simple Stitch (TSS): Insert hook under vertical bar of previous row, yo, draw up a lp.

SCARF
LINK
Make 19.

Row 1: Ch 20, keeping all lps on hook, sk first ch from hook, draw up lp in each rem ch across, do not turn, **RP** (*see Special Stitches*). (20 sts)

Rows 2 & 3: First lp counts as TSS now and throughout, sk first vertical bar, **TSS** (*see Special Stitches*) in each rem vertical bar across, RP. At end of last row, leaving 6-inch end for sewing, fasten off.

Sew ends of first Link together. As each rem Link is made, insert one end through previous Link and then sew ends together. ■

cozy capelet

SKILL LEVEL

EASY

SIZE

One size fits most

FINISHED GARMENT SIZE

16 inches long x 46 inches around bottom edge

MATERIALS

- Noro Kureyon medium (worsted) weight yarn (1¾ oz/110 yds/50g per ball): 3 balls #170 blue/pink/yellow multi
- Size P/Q/15mm crochet hook or size needed to obtain gauge
- Tapestry needle
- Stitch marker

3
LIGHT

GAUGE

8 sc = 4 inches

Take time to check gauge.

PATTERN NOTES

Weave in ends as work progresses.

Join with slip stitch as indicated unless otherwise stated.

CAPELET

Note: Capelet is worked in continuous rounds. Do not join unless specified; mark beginning of rounds.

Rnd 1: Ch 60, **join** (*see Pattern Notes*) in first ch to form a ring, sc in each ch around. Do not join. (*60 sc*)

Rnd 2: Working in **back lps** (*see Stitch Guide*), sc in each sc around.

Rnds 3–6: Rep rnd 2.

Rnd 7: Working through both lps, (2 hdc in next sc, hdc in each of next 4 sc) 12 times. (*72 hdc*)

Rnd 8: (2 hdc in next st, hdc in each of next 5 sts) 12 times. (*84 hdc*)

Rnd 9: Hdc in each st around.

Rnds 10–20: Rep rnd 9.

Rnds 21–24: Rep rnd 2. At end of last rnd, join in beg sc. Fasten off. ■

twisted scarf

SKILL LEVEL

EASY

SIZE
12 inches x 44 inches, unsewn

MATERIALS
- Noro Kogarashi medium (worsted) weight yarn (3½ oz/165 yds/100g per ball): 1 ball #4 purple/lime/salmon
- Size P/Q/15mm crochet hook or size needed to obtain gauge
- Tapestry needle

4 MEDIUM

GAUGE
4 sts = 4 inches

Take time to check gauge.

SCARF
Row 1 (RS): Ch 55, hdc in 3rd ch from hook, hdc in each rem ch across, turn. *(53 hdc)*

Row 2: Ch 2, hdc in each hdc across, turn.

Rep row 2 until piece measures 12 inches from beg. Do not fasten off.

ASSEMBLY
Twist piece once and, holding 2 short ends together, sl st through both thicknesses to form a twisted tube. Fasten off and weave in ends. ■

amelia hat

SKILL LEVEL

■□□ **EASY**

SIZE
One size fits most

FINISHED SIZE
18-inch circumference

MATERIALS
- Noro Silk Garden medium (worsted) weight yarn (1¾ oz/110 yds/50g per ball): 2 balls #309 black/orange/lime
- Size G/6/4mm crochet hook or size needed to obtain gauge
- Tapestry needle

GAUGE
2 shells = 4½ inches; 8 rows = 4 inches

Take time to check gauge.

PATTERN NOTES
Weave in ends as work progresses.

Join with slip stitch as indicated unless otherwise stated.

SPECIAL STITCHES
Shell: (5 dc, ch 1, 5 dc) in indicated sp.

Small shell: (3 dc, ch 1, 3 dc) in indicated sp.

V-st: (Dc, ch 3, dc) in indicated st.

HAT
Foundation rnd: Beg at edge of Hat, ch 8, dc in 4th ch from hook to form lp, (ch 11, dc in 4th ch from hook to form lp) 7 times, ch 3, being careful not to twist ch, **join** (*see Pattern Notes*) in first ch to form ring. (*8 lps*)

Rnd 1: Ch 1, sc in same ch as beg ch-1, **shell** (*see Special Stitches*) in first lp, (sk next 3 chs, sc in next ch, sk next 3 chs, shell in next lp) 7 times, join in beg sc, sl st in each of next 5 dc, sl st in next ch-1 sp, turn. (*8 shells*)

Rnd 2: Ch 1, (sc in ch-1 sp of next shell, ch 3, **V-st**—*see Special Stitches*—in next sc, ch 3) 8 times, join in beg sc, turn. (*8 V-sts*)

Rnd 3: Ch 1, sc in first sc, shell in ch-3 sp of next V-st, (sk next 3 chs, sc in next sc, sk next 3 chs, shell in next lp) 7 times, join in beg sc, sl st in each of next 5 dc, sl st in next ch-1 sp, turn.

Rnds 4 & 5: Rep rnds 2 and 3.

Rnd 6: Ch 1, (sc in ch-1 sp of next shell, ch 2, V-st in next sc, ch 2) 8 times, join in beg sc, turn. (*8 V-sts*)

Rnd 7: Ch 1, sc in first sc, **small shell** (*see Special Stitches*) in ch-3 sp of next V-st, (sk next 3 chs, sc in next sc, sk next 3 chs, small shell in ch-3 sp of next V-st) 7 times, join in beg sc, sl st in each of next 5 dc, sl st in next ch-1 sp, turn.

Rnds 8–13: [Rep rnds 6 and 7 alternately] 3 times. At end of last rnd, fasten off, leaving 12-inch end for sewing.

With tapestry needle, weave end through **back lp** (*see Stitch Guide*) of each st of last rnd, gather to close opening and secure end.

FIRST EAR FLAP
Row 1: Hold Hat with RS facing and foundation rnd at top, join yarn in ch at base of any sc, (shell in ch at base of next shell, sc in ch at base of next sc) twice, turn. (*2 shells*)

Continued on page 45

natalie jacket

SKILL LEVEL

EASY

SIZE

One size fits large–X-large

FINISHED GARMENT SIZE

Center back: 13 inches long
Width around bottom edge: 50 inches

MATERIALS

- Noro Silk Garden Lite light
  (light worsted) weight yarn
  (1¾ oz/137 yds/50g per ball):
    7 balls #3008 blue/green/purple
- Size I/9/5.5mm crochet hook or size
  needed to obtain gauge
- Tapestry needle
- Stitch markers

GAUGE

15 sts and 14 rows = 4 inches

Take time to check gauge.

PATTERN NOTES

Weave in ends as work progresses.

Join with slip stitch as indicated unless
otherwise stated.

Jacket is made in 2 pieces and is different in its
construction, which is why it looks both elegant
and distinctive.

JACKET
FRONT BAND

Row 1: Ch 201, sc in 2nd ch from hook, sc in
each rem ch across, turn. *(200 sc)*

Row 2: Ch 1, sc in first sc, working in **front lps**
(see Stitch Guide), sc in each sc across to last sc,
working through both lps, sc in last sc, turn.

Rows 3–44: Rep row 2. At end of last row,
fasten off.

BACK

*Note: Back is worked sideways beginning at center
back and working to right armhole. Then work from
center back to left armhole.*

RIGHT BACK

Row 1: Ch 51, sc in 2nd ch from hook, sc in each
rem ch across, turn. *(50 sc)*

Row 2: Ch 1, sc in first sc, working in front lps,
sc in each sc across to last sc, working through
both lps, sc in last sc, turn.

Rows 3–44: Rep row 2.

Row 45: Ch 1, working in front lps, sc in each of
first 38 sts, **sc dec** *(see Stitch Guide)* in next 2 sts,
leaving rem sts unworked, turn. *(39 sc)*

Row 46: Ch 1, sk first sc, sc in each rem
sc across, turn. *(38 sc)*

Row 47: Ch 1, working in front lps, sc in each
of first 28 sts, sc dec in next 2 sc, leaving rem
sc unworked, turn. *(29 sc)*

Row 48: Rep row 46. *(28 sc at end of row)*

Row 49: Ch 1, working in front lps, sc in each
of first 23 sc, sc dec in next 2 sc, leaving rem
sc unworked. Fasten off.

LEFT BACK

Row 1: Hold piece with foundation ch at top
and last st of row 49 at left-hand edge, **join**
(see Pattern Notes) in first ch of foundation ch,
ch 1, sc in same ch as beg ch-1, sc in each rem
ch across, turn. *(50 sc)*

Rows 2–49: Rep rows 2–49 of Right Back.

Continued on page 46

stripy skirt

SKILL LEVEL
◧■◻◻
EASY

SIZES
Instructions given fit size small; changes for medium are in [ ].

FINISHED GARMENT SIZES
Hips: 32 inches (*small*); 36 inches (*medium*)

MATERIALS
- Noro Silk Garden Lite light (light worsted) weight yarn (1¾ oz/137 yds/50g per ball): 6 (7) balls #2012 olive/purples/salmon
- Size F/5/3.75mm crochet hook or size needed to obtain gauge
- Tapestry needle
- Sewing needle
- 1 yd ¼-inch-wide elastic
- 1-inch buttons: 4
- Matching sewing thread

GAUGE
19 dc and 10 rows = 4 inches

Take time to check gauge.

PATTERN NOTES
Weave in ends as work progresses.

Join with slip stitch as indicated unless otherwise stated.

Single crochet and chain-1 at beginning of row counts as a double crochet unless otherwise stated.

Work all stitches in **front lps** (*see Stitch Guide*) unless otherwise stated.

SKIRT
FRONT/BACK
Make 2.

Notes: *Make 2 pieces beginning at bottom and work toward waist. Work center front and center back bands directly onto one piece. Then sew on 2nd side to form a shaped tube.*

Row 1: Ch 86 [92], sc in 2nd ch from hook, sc in each rem ch across, turn. (*85 [91] sc*)

Row 2: Ch 1, (sc, ch 1) in first sc (*see Pattern Notes*), dc in each rem sc across, turn.

Row 3: Ch 1, sc in each dc across to ch-1, sc in ch-1, turn. (*85 [91] sc*)

Rep rows 2 and 3 until piece measures 13½ [14] inches from beg.

DART SHAPING
Row 1: Sk first sc, (sc, ch 1) in next sc, dc in each of next 26 [28] sc, **dc dec** (*see Stitch Guide*) in next 2 sc, dc in each of next 25 [27] sc, dc dec in next 2 sc, dc in each of next 26 [28] dc, dc dec in last 2 sc, turn. (*81 [87] dc*)

Row 2: Ch 1, sc in each dc across to ch-1, sc in ch-1, turn.

Row 3: Sk first sc, (sc, ch 1) in next sc, dc in each of next 25 [27] sc, dc dec in next 2 sc, dc in each of next 23 [25] sc, dc dec in next 2 sc, dc in each of next 25 [27] sc, dc dec in last 2 sc, turn. (*77 [83] dc*)

Row 4: Rep row 2.

Row 5: Sk first sc, (sc, ch 1) in next sc, dc in each of next 24 [26] sc, dc dec in next 2 sc, dc in each of next 21 [23] sc, dc dec in next 2 sc, dc in each of next 24 [26] sc, dc dec in last 2 sc, turn. *(73 [79] dc)*

Row 6: Rep row 2.

Row 7: Sk first sc, (sc, ch 1) in next sc, dc in each of next 23 [25] sc, dc dec in next 2 sc, dc in each of next 19 [21] sc, dc dec in next 2 sc, dc in each of next 23 [25] sc, dc dec in last 2 sc, turn. *(69 [75] dc)*

Row 8: Rep row 2.

Row 9: Sk first sc, (sc, ch 1) in next sc, dc in each of next 22 [24] sc, dc dec in next 2 sc, dc in each of next 17 [19] sc, dc dec in next 2 sc, dc in each of next 22 [24] sc, dc dec in last 2 sc, turn. *(65 [71] dc)*

Rows 10–12: Rep row 2. At end of last row, fasten off.

CENTER FRONT BAND

Row 1: Hold 1 piece with last row worked at right-hand edge, join yarn in side of last row, ch 1, sc in same sp, working in ends of rows, sc evenly sp across edge, turn.

Row 2: Ch 1, working in **front lps** *(see Stitch Guide)*, sc in each sc across to last sc, sc through both lps of last sc, turn.

Rows 3–5: Rep row 2. At end of last row, fasten off.

CENTER BACK BAND

Row 1: Hold piece with opposite long edge at top, join yarn in side of first row at right-hand edge, ch 1, sc in same sp, working in ends of rows, sc evenly sp across edge, turn.

Rows 2–5: Rep rows 2–5 of Center Front Band.

ASSEMBLY

Sew long sides of Center Bands to long sides of 2nd piece, forming tube. Cut a piece of elastic 2 inches shorter than waist width. Overlap ends and sew together to form ring.

WAIST EDGING

Join *(see Pattern Notes)* yarn in 1 seam at top of Skirt, ch 1, holding elastic behind work and working over elastic, sc in each st around and in each seam, join in beg sc. Fasten off.

HEM EDGING

Row 1: Hold Skirt with bottom edge at top, join yarn in 1 seam, ch 2, (sc, ch 1) in each ch sp around to beg ch-2, sc in beg ch-2 sp, turn.

Row 2: Ch 2, (sc, ch 1) in each ch-1 sp around to beg ch-2 sp, sc in beg ch-2 sp. Fasten off.

FINISHING

Referring to photo for placement, sew buttons to Center Front Band. ∎

light layers vest

Continued from page 6

Rep on 2nd long edge.

ARMHOLE EDGING

Rnd 1: With size G hook, join yarn in edge of 1 armhole, *ch 1, sc in same sp, ch 1, sk next row, sc in next row, taking care to keep edge flat, rep from * around, join in beg sc.

Rnd 2: Ch 2, (sc, ch 1) in each ch-1 sp around, join in beg ch-2 sp.

Rnd 3: Ch 2, (sc, ch 1) in each ch-1 sp around, join in beg ch-2 sp. Fasten off.

Rep on 2nd armhole. ■

aztec shawl

Continued from page 11

Rows 96–101: [Rep rows 10 and 11 alternately] 3 times.

Row 102: Ch 3, (3 dc, ch 1) in each of next 12 ch-1 sps, 3 dc in next ch-1 sp, leaving rem ch-1 sps unworked, turn. *(13 groups of 3 dc)*

Row 103: Ch 4, sk next 3 dc, (3 dc, ch 1) in each of next 12 ch-1 sps, dc in 3rd ch of beg ch-3, turn.

Rows 104–109: [Rep rows 10 and 11 alternately] 3 times.

Row 110: Ch 3, (3 dc, ch 1) in each of next 6 ch-1 sps, 3 dc in next ch-1 sp, leaving rem ch-1 sps unworked, turn. *(7 groups of 3 dc)*

Row 111: Ch 4, sk next 3 dc, (3 dc, ch 1) in each of next 6 ch-1 sps, dc in 3rd ch of beg ch-3, turn. *(6 groups of 3 dc)*

Rows 112–117: [Rep rows 10 and 11 alternately] 3 times.

EDGING

Rnd 1: Hold Shawl with foundation ch at top, **join** *(see Pattern Notes)* in first ch, ch 1, working around outer edge, sc evenly sp around outer edge, working 3 sc in each outside corner and working **cl** *(see Special Stitch)* in each inside corner, join in beg sc.

Rnd 2: Working in **back lps** *(see Stitch Guide)*, sc in each sc around, working outside corner sts through both lps and inside corners as before, join in beg sc.

Rnds 3–5: Rep rnd 2. At end of last rnd, fasten off. ■

dolman sleeve lacy shrug

Continued from page 12

LEFT FRONT

Begin at the forearm and work to the neck opening.

Row 1: Beg at sleeve edge, ch 37, (dc, ch 3, dc) in 6th ch from hook, *sk next 3 chs, (dc, ch 3, dc) in next ch, rep from * across to last 3 chs, sk next 2 chs, dc in last ch, turn. *(8 V-sts)*

Row 2: Ch 4, [shell in next ch-3 sp, ch 1] across to sp formed by beg 5 sk chs, dc in sp formed by beg 5 sk chs, turn. *(8 shells)*

Row 3: Ch 6, dc in next ch-1 sp, V-st in each rem ch-1 sp across to last ch-1 sp, (dc, ch 3, dc) in last ch-1 sp, turn.

Row 4: Ch 4, shell in first ch-3 sp, ch 1, [shell in next ch-3 sp, ch 1] across to ch-6 sp, (shell, ch 1, dc) in ch-6 sp, turn. *(9 shells)*

Rows 5–20: Rep [rows 3 and 4 alternately] 8 times. *(17 shells at end of last row)*

Row 21: Rep row 3.

Row 22: Ch 4, shell in next ch-3 sp, ch 1, [shell in next ch-3 sp, ch 1] across to ch-6 sp, (shell, ch 1, 2 dc, ch 1, dc) in last ch-6 sp, turn.

Row 23: Rep row 3.

Row 24: Rep row 22.

Row 25: Rep row 3.

Row 26: Rep row 22.

Row 27: Rep row 3.

Row 28: Ch 4, shell in next ch-3 sp, ch 1, [shell in next ch-3 sp, ch 1] across to ch-6 sp, (shell, ch 1, dc) in ch-6 sp, turn. Fasten off. *(24 shells)*

RIGHT FRONT

Rows 1–21: Rep rows 1–21 of Left Front.

Row 22: Ch 4, (2 dc, ch 1, shell) in next ch-3 sp, ch 1, [shell in next ch-3 sp, ch 1] across to last ch-6 sp, (shell, ch 1, dc) in last ch-6 sp, turn.

Row 23: Rep row 3.

Row 24: Rep row 22.

Row 25: Rep row 3.

Row 26: Rep row 22.

Row 27: Rep row 3.

Row 28: Ch 4, shell in next ch-3 sp, ch 1, [shell in next ch-3 sp, ch 1] across to ch-6 sp, (shell, ch 1, dc) in ch-6 sp. Fasten off. *(24 shells)*

ASSEMBLY

Sew center back seam. Sew shoulder seams. For first side seam, join yarn with sc through both thickness at bottom edge, *ch 3, sk ½ inch, sc through both thicknesses, rep from * across side. Rep for 2nd side seam. Sew sleeve seams in same manner.

BACK NECK EDGING

Row 1: Holding Shrug with RS facing, **join** *(see Pattern Notes)* yarn in shoulder seam at right-hand edge, ch 2, (sc, ch 1) evenly sp across to next shoulder seam, sc in shoulder seam, turn.

Row 2: Ch 2, (sc, ch 1) in each ch-1 sp across to last ch-2 sp, sc in last ch-2 sp, turn.

Rows 3 & 4: Rep row 2.

OUTER EDGING

Rnd 1: Ch 1, sc in first sc, *ch 5, sk ½ inch, sc in next st or sp, rep from * around entire outer edge to beg sc, ch 2, join with dc in beg sc.

Rnd 2: *Ch 5, sc in next ch-5 sp, rep from * around, ch 2, join with dc in joining dc.

Rnd 3: *(Ch 5, sc in next ch-5 sp) 3 times, ch 5, sc in next ch-5 sp, rep from * around, ch 2, join with dc in joining dc.

Rnds 4–8: Rep rnd 2.

Rnd 9: Ch 1, sc in same st as beg ch-1, *5 dc in next sc, (sc in next ch-5 sp, ch 5) twice, sc in next ch-5 sp, rep from * around, adjusting last rep as necessary to end evenly, join in first sc. Fasten off.

SLEEVE EDGING

Note: Cut 2 lengths of elastic, each 11 inches long. For each length, overlap ends ½ inch and sew together to form ring.

Rnd 1: Hold one Sleeve edge with RS facing and 1 elastic ring behind work, join yarn in seam, ch 1, working over elastic, sc evenly sp around edge, join in beg sc.

Rnd 2: Ch 1, working over elastic again, sc in each sc, join in beg sc.

Rnd 3: Ch 1, sc in same ch as beg ch-1, *ch 5, sk ½ inch, sc in next dc, rep from * around to beg sc, ch 2, join with dc in first sc.

Rnds 4–11: Rep rnds 2–9 of Outer Edging. ■

crisscross vest
Continued from page 15

Row 7: Ch 3, V-st in each of first 8 ch-1 sps, (2 V-sts in next ch-1 sp, V-st in next ch-1 sp) 12 times, V-st in each of last 12 ch-1 sps, dc in 3rd ch of turning ch-3, turn. *(56 V-sts)*

Row 8: Ch 3, V-st in each ch-1 sp across, dc in 3rd ch of turning ch-3, turn.

Rows 9 & 10: Rep row 8.

Row 11: Ch 3, V-st in each of first 8 ch-1 sps, (2 V-sts in next ch-1 sp, V-st in each of next 2 ch-1 sps) 12 times, V-st in each of last 12 ch-1 sps, dc in 3rd ch of turning ch-3, turn. *(68 V-sts)*

Rows 12–14: Rep row 8.

Row 15: Ch 3, V-st in each of first 8 ch-1 sps, (2 V-sts in next ch-1 sp, V-st in each of next 3 ch-1 sps) 12 times, V-st in each of last 12 ch-1 sps, dc in 3rd ch of turning ch-3, turn. *(80 V-sts)*

Rows 16–18: Rep row 8.

Row 19: Ch 3, V-st in each of first 8 ch-1 sps, (2 V-sts in next ch-1 sp, V-st in each of next 4 ch-1 sps) 12 times, V-st in each of last 12 ch-1 sps, dc in 3rd ch of turning ch-3, turn. *(92 V-sts)*

Rows 20–22: Rep row 8.

Row 23: Ch 2, sk next st, *sc in next st, ch 1, sk next st, rep from * across to last st, sc in last st. Fasten off.

ASSEMBLY
Referring to diagrams, sew collar seam. Sew edge of Side 1 to collar, matching points D–A on each piece. Rep with edge of Side 2, sewing points A–D to same points on Side 1. ■

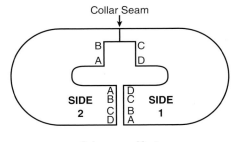

Crisscross Vest
Assembly Diagram

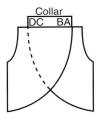

Crisscross Vest
Back View

lyndalls cardigan

Continued from page 26

SLEEVE
Make 2.

Row 1: With size P hook, ch 30 [34], sc in 4th ch from hook, *ch 1, sk next ch, sc in next ch, rep from * across, turn.

Row 2: Ch 2, [sc in next ch-1 sp, ch 1] across to sp formed by beg 3 sk chs, sc in same sp, turn.

Row 3: Ch 2, [sc in next ch-1 sp, ch 1] across to ch-2 sp, sc in same ch-2 sp, turn.

Row 4: Rep row 3.

Row 5 (inc row): Ch 2, sc in first sc, ch 1, sc in next ch-1 sp, [ch 1, sk next sc, sc in next ch-1 sp] across to ch-2 sp, (sc, ch 1, sc) in ch-2 sp, turn.

Rows 6–14: Rep row 3.

Row 15: Rep row 5.

Rows 16–19: Rep row 3.

Row 20: Rep row 5.

Rows 21–24: Rep row 3. At end of last row, fasten off.

ASSEMBLY
Sew shoulder seams. Sew Sleeves into armholes; then sew side and sleeve seams.

EDGING
Hold Cardigan with RS facing and bottom edge at top, with size N hook, join yarn with a sc in ch at center back of foundation ch, sc in each ch to right front corner, 3 sc in corner, sc evenly sp along right front to top corner, (sc, ch 10, sc) in corner *(button loop made)*, sc evenly sp along neck edge to left front top corner, 3 sc in corner, sc evenly sp along left front to bottom corner, 3 sc in corner, working across bottom edge, sc in each ch across to beg sc, join with sl st in beg sc. Fasten off.

FINISHING
Sew button opposite button loop. ■

amelia hat

Continued from page 35

Row 2: Sl st in each of next 5 dc and in next ch-1 sp, ch 1, sc in same sp, ch 2, V-st in next sc, ch 2, sc in next ch-1 sp, turn.

Row 3: Ch 1, sc in first sc, small shell in ch-3 sp of next V-st, sc in last sc. Fasten off.

2ND EAR FLAP
Row 1: Sk ch at base of each of next 2 shells from First Ear Flap, join yarn in ch at base of next sc, (shell in ch at base of next shell, sc in ch at base of next sc) twice, turn. *(2 shells)*

Row 2: Sl st in each of next 5 dc and in next ch-1 sp, ch 1, sc in same sp, ch 2, V-st in next sc, ch 2, sc in next ch-1 sp, turn.

Row 3: Ch 1, sc in first sc, small shell in ch-3 sp of next V-st, sc in last sc. Do not fasten off.

EDGING
Rnd 1: Ch 2, [sc, ch 1] down side of ear flap, across edge and up side of next ear flap to shell at top, (sc, ch 1, sc) in ch-3 sp of shell, [sc, ch 1] down side of ear flap, across edge and up side of next ear flap to shell at top, (sc, ch 1, sc) in ch-3 sp of shell, join in beg sc, turn.

Rnd 2: Ch 2, [sc in next ch-1 sp, ch 1] around to beg ch-2 sp, sc in beg ch-2 sp, turn.

Rnd 3: Rep rnd 2. At end of rnd, fasten off. ■

natalie jacket

Continued from page 36

ASSEMBLY

Place stitch markers to divide Front Band as shown on diagram. Sew first 25 sts to underarm on Back. Leave 25 sts unsewn for armhole opening. Sew next 100 sts to top of Back. Leave next 25 sts unsewn for 2nd armhole opening. Sew last 25 sts to the other underarm on Back.

LOWER EDGING

Row 1: Hold bottom edge of Jacket at top, join yarn in first st at right-hand corner, ch 1, sc in same st as beg ch-1, sc in each st across, turn.

Row 2: Ch 1, sc in each sc across, turn.

Rows 3–11: Rep row 2. At end of last row, fasten off.

FRONT EDGING

Row 1: Hold Jacket with RS facing and right front opening at top, join yarn in side of first row at right-hand edge, ch 2, working in ends of rows, [sc, ch 1] evenly sp across right front to top corner, (sc, ch 1, sc) in corner, [sc, ch 1] evenly sp across neck edge to left top corner, (sc, ch 1, sc) in corner, working across left front in ends of rows, [sc, ch 1] evenly sp across to last row, turn.

Row 2: Ch 2, [sc in next ch-1 sp, ch 1] across to last ch-2 sp, sc in last ch-2 sp, turn.

Rows 3–5: Rep row 2. At end of last row, fasten off. ■

Joins with B	25 sts		Joins with C		25 sts	Joins with A
25 sts	Armhole Do not stitch		100 sts		Armhole Do not stitch	25 sts

Natalie Jacket
Assembly Diagram

Natalie Jacket
Back

STITCH GUIDE

FOR MORE COMPLETE INFORMATION,
VISIT **ANNIESCATALOG.COM/STITCHGUIDE**

STITCH ABBREVIATIONS

beg	begin/begins/beginning
bpdc	back post double crochet
bpsc	back post single crochet
bptr	back post treble crochet
CC	contrasting color
ch(s)	chain(s)
ch-	refers to chain or space previously made (i.e., ch-1 space)
ch sp(s)	chain space(s)
cl(s)	cluster(s)
cm	centimeter(s)
dc	double crochet (singular/plural)
dc dec	double crochet 2 or more stitches together, as indicated
dec	decrease/decreases/decreasing
dtr	double treble crochet
ext	extended
fpdc	front post double crochet
fpsc	front post single crochet
fptr	front post treble crochet
g	gram(s)
hdc	half double crochet
hdc dec	half double crochet 2 or more stitches together, as indicated
inc	increase/increases/increasing
lp(s)	loop(s)
MC	main color
mm	millimeter(s)
oz	ounce(s)
pc	popcorn(s)
rem	remain/remains/remaining
rep(s)	repeat(s)
rnd(s)	round(s)
RS	right side
sc	single crochet (singular/plural)
sc dec	single crochet 2 or more stitches together, as indicated
sk	skip/skipped/skipping
sl st(s)	slip stitch(es)
sp(s)	space(s)/spaced
st(s)	stitch(es)
tog	together
tr	treble crochet
trtr	triple treble
WS	wrong side
yd(s)	yard(s)
yo	yarn over

YARN CONVERSION

OUNCES TO GRAMS		GRAMS TO OUNCES	
1	28.4	25	7/8
2	56.7	40	1 2/3
3	85.0	50	1 3/4
4	113.4	100	3 1/2

UNITED STATES		UNITED KINGDOM
sl st (slip stitch)	=	sc (single crochet)
sc (single crochet)	=	dc (double crochet)
hdc (half double crochet)	=	htr (half treble crochet)
dc (double crochet)	=	tr (treble crochet)
tr (treble crochet)	=	dtr (double treble crochet)
dtr (double treble crochet)	=	ttr (triple treble crochet)
skip	=	miss

Single crochet decrease (sc dec): (Insert hook, yo, draw lp through) in each of the sts indicated, yo, draw through all lps on hook.

Example of 2-sc dec

Half double crochet decrease (hdc dec): (Yo, insert hook, yo, draw lp through) in each of the sts indicated, yo, draw through all lps on hook.

Example of 2-hdc dec

Reverse single crochet (reverse sc): Ch 1, sk first st, working from left to right, insert hook in next st from front to back, draw up lp on hook, yo and draw through both lps on hook.

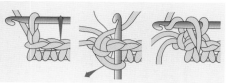

Chain (ch): Yo, pull through lp on hook.

Single crochet (sc): Insert hook in st, yo, pull through st, yo, pull through both lps on hook.

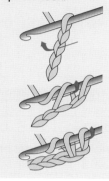

Double crochet (dc): Yo, insert hook in st, yo, pull through st, [yo, pull through 2 lps] twice.

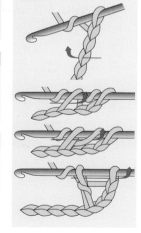

Double crochet decrease (dc dec): (Yo, insert hook, yo, draw lp through, yo, draw through 2 lps on hook) in each of the sts indicated, yo, draw through all lps on hook.

Example of 2-dc dec

Front loop (front lp) Back loop (back lp)

Front Loop   Back Loop

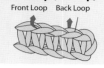

Front post stitch (fp): Back post stitch (bp): When working post st, insert hook from right to left around post of st on previous row.

Back   Front

Post of Stitch

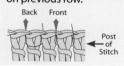

Half double crochet (hdc): Yo, insert hook in st, yo, pull through st, yo, pull through all 3 lps on hook.

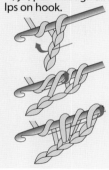

Double treble crochet (dtr): Yo 3 times, insert hook in st, yo, pull through st, [yo, pull through 2 lps] 4 times.

Treble crochet decrease (tr dec): Holding back last lp of each st, tr in each of the sts indicated, yo, pull through all lps on hook.

Example of 2-tr dec

Slip stitch (sl st): Insert hook in st, pull through both lps on hook.

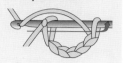

Chain color change (ch color change) Yo with new color, draw through last lp on hook.

Double crochet color change (dc color change) Drop first color, yo with new color, draw through last 2 lps of st.

Treble crochet (tr): Yo twice, insert hook in st, yo, pull through st, [yo, pull through 2 lps] 3 times.

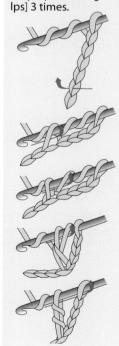

Metric Conversion Charts

METRIC CONVERSIONS

yards	x	.9144	=	metres (m)
yards	x	91.44	=	centimetres (cm)
inches	x	2.54	=	centimetres (cm)
inches	x	25.40	=	millimetres (mm)
inches	x	.0254	=	metres (m)

centimetres	x	.3937	=	inches
metres	x	1.0936	=	yards

INCHES INTO MILLIMETRES & CENTIMETRES (Rounded off slightly)

inches	mm	cm	inches	cm	inches	cm	inches	cm
1/8	3	0.3	5	12.5	21	53.5	38	96.5
1/4	6	0.6	5 1/2	14	22	56	39	99
3/8	10	1	6	15	23	58.5	40	101.5
1/2	13	1.3	7	18	24	61	41	104
5/8	15	1.5	8	20.5	25	63.5	42	106.5
3/4	20	2	9	23	26	66	43	109
7/8	22	2.2	10	25.5	27	68.5	44	112
1	25	2.5	11	28	28	71	45	114.5
1 1/4	32	3.2	12	30.5	29	73.5	46	117
1 1/2	38	3.8	13	33	30	76	47	119.5
1 3/4	45	4.5	14	35.5	31	79	48	122
2	50	5	15	38	32	81.5	49	124.5
2 1/2	65	6.5	16	40.5	33	84	50	127
3	75	7.5	17	43	34	86.5		
3 1/2	90	9	18	46	35	89		
4	100	10	19	48.5	36	91.5		
4 1/2	115	11.5	20	51	37	94		

KNITTING NEEDLES CONVERSION CHART

Canada/U.S.	0	1	2	3	4	5	6	7	8	9	10	10½	11	13	15
Metric (mm)	2	2¼	2¾	3¼	3½	3¾	4	4½	5	5½	6	6½	8	9	10

CROCHET HOOKS CONVERSION CHART

Canada/U.S.	1/B	2/C	3/D	4/E	5/F	6/G	8/H	9/I	10/J	10½/K	N
Metric (mm)	2.25	2.75	3.25	3.5	3.75	4.25	5	5.5	6	6.5	9.0

Annie's®

Fashions to Flaunt is published by Annie's, 306 East Parr Road, Berne, IN 46711. Printed in USA. Copyright © 2012, 2013 Annie's. All rights reserved. This publication may not be reproduced in part or in whole without written permission from the publisher.

RETAIL STORES: If you would like to carry this pattern book or any other Annie's publication, visit AnniesWSL.com.

Every effort has been made to ensure that the instructions in this pattern book are complete and accurate. We cannot, however, take responsibility for human error, typographical mistakes or variations in individual work. Please visit AnniesCustomerCare.com to check for pattern updates.

ISBN: 978-1-59635-710-5

3 4 5 6 7 8 9